LET'S FIND OUT! ENGINEERING

SOLVING REAL-WORLD PROBLEMS WITH ENVIRONMENTAL AND GREEN ENGINEERING

KRISTI LEW

Britannica®
Educational Publishing

IN ASSOCIATION WITH

ROSEN
EDUCATIONAL SERVICES

T0026228

Published in 2016 by Britannica Educational Publishing (a trademark of Encyclopædia Britannica, Inc.) in association with The Rosen Publishing Group, Inc.
29 East 21st Street, New York, NY 10010

Distributed exclusively by Rosen Publishing.
To see additional Britannica Educational Publishing titles, go to rosenpublishing.com.

First Edition

Britannica Educational Publishing
J.E. Luebering: Director, Core Reference Group
Mary Rose McCudden: Editor, Britannica Student Encyclopedia

Rosen Publishing
Kathy Kuhtz Campbell: Senior Editor
Nelson Sá: Art Director
Nicole Russo: Designer
Cindy Reiman: Photography Manager
Karen Huang: Photo Researcher

Library of Congress Cataloging-in-Publication Data
Lew, Kristi, author.
Solving real-world problems with environmental and green engineering / Kristi Lew.
   pages cm. — (Let's find out! Engineering)
Includes bibliographical references and index.
Audience: Grades 1–4.
ISBN 978-1-68048-264-5 (library bound) — ISBN 978-1-5081-0075-1 (pbk.) — ISBN 978-1-68048-321-5 (6-pack)
1. Environmental engineering—Juvenile literature. 2. Green technology—Juvenile literature. 3. Sustainable engineering—Juvenile literature. I. Title.
TA170.L48 2016
628—dc23
                                                                    201502672

Manufactured in the United States of America

Photo credits: Cover, p. 1, interior pages background image artjazz/Shutterstock.com; pp. 4, 6, 21, 27 © AP Images; p. 5 Thomas Fredberg/Science Source; p. 7 BanksPhotos/E+/Getty Images; p. 8 Monty Rakusen/Cultura/Getty Images; p. 9 Justin Sullivan/Getty Images; p. 10 Patrick Pleul/picture-alliance/dpa/AP Images; p. 11 ChinaFotoPress/Getty Images; p. 12 Gilles Bassignac/Gamma-Rapho/Getty Images; p. 13 Dieter Spannknebel/Stockbyte/Getty Images; p. 14 Insights/Universal Images Group/Getty Images; p. 15 Yvette Cardozo/Photographer's Choice/Getty Images; pp. 16, 26 Bloomberg/Getty Images; p. 17 Peter Bennett/Ambient Images/Newscom; p. 18 Stephanie Bidouze/Shutterstock.com; p. 19 Glenn Cantor/Moment/Getty Images; p. 20 Spencer Grant/Science Source; p. 22 Cultura RM/Georgia Kuhn/Getty Images; p. 23 Thorsten Henn/Cultura/Getty Images; p. 24 Michael Layefsky/Moment/Getty Images; p. 25 KGlavin/Wikimedia Commons: File: Crystal Springs Dam Front.jpg/CC BY 2.5; p. 28 Erin Siegal/Redux.

CONTENTS

THE GREEN TEAM

Engineers are people who use their knowledge of science to fix problems. They produce things that can make life easy, safe, or fun. To do this, they might use their skills to improve an object or they might invent something new.

Lots of engineers use a method called green engineering. The purpose of green engineering is to help protect the land, water, and air that make up Earth's environment. Some engineers practice green engineering by deciding to use building and power supplies that are safe

Engineers invented a car engine that can run on used cooking oil.

An engineer works on a bus that will run on both electricity and a fuel called diesel fuel.

and plentiful. Others apply green engineering by cutting down on waste and the use of natural resources. These practices allow an engineer's inventions to be made for many years to come.

Natural resources are things found in nature that can be used by people. They include air, water, plants, oil, and soil.

Waste Not, Want Not

Many people are worried that humans are using too many of the world's natural resources. One way to save natural resources is to reuse them instead of throwing them away. Engineers have found many ways to recycle old things.

For example, engineers planning new buildings might use the wood or metal from old buildings that have been torn down. They could also decide to make the building's deck out of lumber made from old plastic bottles

These students are making new paper out of recycled paper.

Insulation made from recycled blue jeans is used in walls of homes.

instead of wood. Old blue jeans can be used to make insulation for a building. The metal parts on windows and doors can be made from old cans. Old glass bottles can be ground up and turned into glass blocks. In these ways, many of the things people use every day can be reused and not wasted.

THINK ABOUT IT

Engineers are not the only ones who can cut down on the amount of waste. What are some of the ways you and your family could limit waste in your home?

POWER TO THE PEOPLE

Engineers save natural resources by reusing old things. They also save resources by not using them at all. People need power to run their cars, heat their homes, and light their streets and buildings. Oil, coal, and gas are natural resources people use to make power.

Coal is dug from the ground to be used as fuel.

Oil, coal, and natural gas are called fossil fuels. It takes hundreds of millions of years for fossil fuels to form. Because people use them much faster than they can form, the fossil fuels on Earth are in short supply. Engineers practicing green engineering try to use these limited supplies as little as possible.

Sunlight, wind, and water are also natural resources that can be used as power supplies. Unlike fossil fuels,

Fossil fuels are energy sources formed from the remains of living things that died hundreds of millions of years ago.

Some cars can run on biofuel such as biodiesel made from plant or animal materials.

Engineers check the blades of a large windmill.

these power sources cannot be used up. For this reason, they are called renewable energy sources.

Engineers try to use renewable energy sources whenever possible. For example, they have made cars and trucks that can run on used cooking oil or other

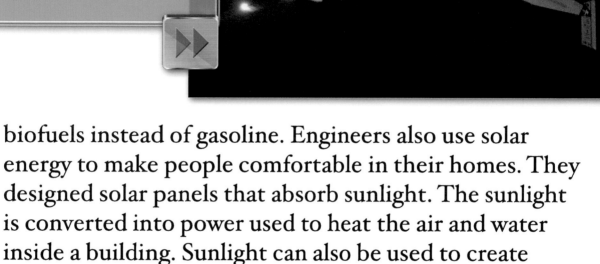

This solar-powered airplane runs on energy gathered from the sun.

biofuels instead of gasoline. Engineers also use solar energy to make people comfortable in their homes. They designed solar panels that absorb sunlight. The sunlight is converted into power used to heat the air and water inside a building. Sunlight can also be used to create electricity.

COMPARE AND CONTRAST

Compare and contrast gasoline and solar power. Which is more likely to remain easy to get in the coming years?

It's Getting Hot in Here!

Running out of fossil fuels is not the only problem people may face if they continue to use these power sources. Burning fossil fuels also adds carbon dioxide gas to the air. Scientists believe a rise in the amount of this gas in Earth's atmosphere is the cause of global warming.

Global warming is the slow rise in Earth's average temperature.

Harmful gases are given off when power plants burn fossil fuels.

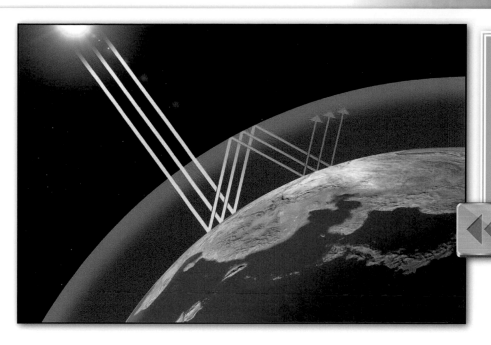

Greenhouse gases trap heat inside Earth's atmosphere.

To understand global warming, it helps to understand the greenhouse effect. A greenhouse is a glass house where plants grow. Glass lets light in and keeps heat from escaping. This trapped heat keeps the plants warm even when it is cold outside.

Likewise, Earth's atmosphere traps energy from the sun. Carbon dioxide and other gases—called greenhouse gases—in the air do this trapping.

Without these gases, too much heat would go back into space and living things could not survive. However, as more greenhouse gases get into the air, they also trap more heat.

Warmer conditions could harm living things. They also could cause polar ice caps to melt. The melted ice would cause sea levels to rise. Plants, animals, and buildings along coastlines would be in danger.

Engineers are trying to find ways to limit the amount of greenhouse gases put into the air. Using renewable energy sources instead of fossil fuels is one way they can do this. Many engineers plan projects that use wind or solar power instead of gas and oil. Engineers are also

As Earth warms, icebergs and glaciers melt.

Rooftop gardens remove carbon dioxide from the air while supplying people with fresh food.

searching for ways to take greenhouse gases out of the air. Plants take in carbon dioxide to make their own food. Therefore, some engineers plan buildings that can support rooftop gardens and walls covered in plants.

THINK ABOUT IT

Most power plants burn fossil fuels to make electricity. Some engineers put wind catchers in buildings to help cool the air inside. How could this plan help slow down global warming?

LET'S CLEAN UP

Not only does burning fossil fuels add greenhouse gases to the air, but it may also add ash and soot. Ash and soot are forms of air pollution. They turn buildings and statues black and can cause people to get sick. To fix this problem, engineers have invented machines called scrubbers. Scrubbers take ash, soot, and gases given off by power plants out of the air. Engineers have also come up with systems to cut down on the pollution given off by cars and trucks. One way they cut down on pollution is by making cars that use less gasoline.

Hybrid cars can run on electricity as well as gasoline.

Waste, chemicals, and other harmful things can also pollute the land and water. Littering, or tossing garbage on the ground, is one form of land pollution. The buildup of unsafe chemicals in the soil is another. Some engineers work to find new ways to use the waste people throw away. Plastic bottles, for example, can be turned into clothing, outdoor furniture, and flooring for people's homes.

THINK ABOUT IT

Think about the things you do every day. How could you help stop air and land pollution?

Old plastic bottles can be used to make new tables and chairs.

Trash is ugly, and it can harm animals that live in the water.

Some causes of water pollution are easy to see. People dump garbage into creeks, rivers, ponds, lakes, and oceans. Factories or cities sometimes release oils, poisonous chemicals, and other wastes into water.

Engineers have invented different ways to clean polluted waters. Sometimes they use screens, or filters, to take out trash, rocks, and dirt. Oil and chemicals can be harder to get rid of. However, engineers have found that they can use living things — such as earthworms,

Earthworms can help clean up some harmful chemicals.

fungi, and bacteria—to solve this problem. These organisms can break down oil and some of the other things that pollute the water. They can also break down chemicals that have built up in the soil.

Compare and Contrast

Compare and contrast the use of filters and the use of bacteria to remove pollution. Why do you think bacteria are used instead of filters in some cases?

Green Centered

Although many engineers practice green engineering, some pay special attention to making people's surroundings cleaner and safer. These engineers are called environmental engineers. They think about ways to fix environmental problems.

For example, environmental engineers might work to make sure everyone in a town has safe drinking water. They plan how water will get to people's homes, schools, and businesses.

Engineers work on a plan to turn dirty water into clean water so that it can be reused.

They map out ways to take dirty water away from these places, too. They also invent safe methods to clean the dirty water.

Environmental engineers might also plan how and where people throw away their trash. They make sure that people's waste does not pollute the surrounding water or land. They also take part in cleaning up spaces that have been polluted in the past.

Engineers invented this machine to help contain oil that spilled into the Gulf of Mexico.

COMPARE AND CONTRAST

Compare and contrast environmental engineers and engineers who practice green engineering. In what ways do both types of engineers keep Earth and the people who live here safe?

Planning for Tomorrow

Imagine that a group of people would like to build a city. The land where they want to build it is covered in trees and grass. They ask an engineer to help them find the best way to build their city. **Urban planning** is how engineers can help cities plan for the future. An engineer is likely to suggest that the city leaders leave behind some of the trees, grasses, and other

Urban planning is a way to balance the needs of people with the needs of the environment.

Engineers help city leaders make plans to rebuild parts of a city.

plants. These living things create green space in the city. Green spaces take in greenhouse gases from the air. They also give people places to rest and play.

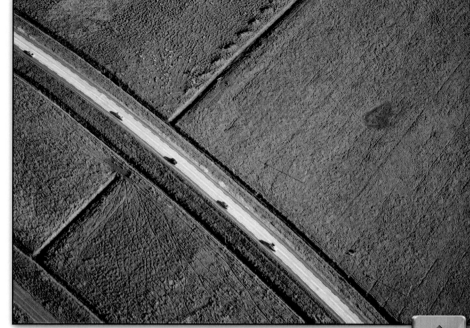

Something else an engineer might suggest is using ground covers that

Rainwater that runs off a highway may be polluted. Growing plants along roads helps clean the water.

let rainwater through. Such a covering lets water drip slowly into the dirt instead of running off the sides of the pavement all at once. The dirt acts as a filter that cleans pollution out of the rainwater.

Keep It Going

When planning a city, engineers think about the best ways to get clean water to people's homes, schools, and businesses. They also decide how to take dirty water and other waste away. They consider the best places to put recycling centers. They study how to do all of that while using the smallest amount of energy and natural resources. These practices let engineers plan for sustainable growth. Sustainable growth means a city can get bigger without using up or dirtying its natural resources.

Sustainable means that something can go on and on.

Water cleaning plants are often placed at the edges of a city.

24

One example of how engineers might make a city's water supply sustainable is by studying the best place they can build it. They need to make sure the water supply is far away from garbage dumps or other places that might pollute the water. But they also need to make sure the water is not so far away that it takes extra resources to get it where it needs to go.

The placement of a city's water source is very important.

ENGINEERING IN ACTION

In everything they do, engineers try to solve people's problems. By using green engineering, they can make solutions without hurting Earth. Sometimes, these answers mean that engineers will imagine a way to improve something that already exists. Instead of building a new car that burns fossil fuels, an engineer might design one that uses batteries. At other times, an engineer might make the world a better place by inventing a new machine.

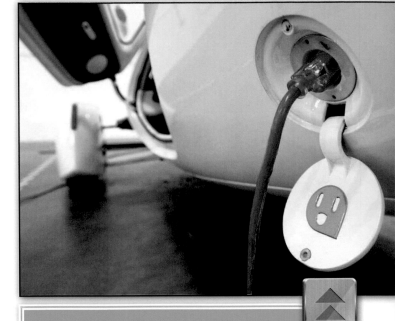

An electric car stores energy in its batteries. It runs on electricity instead of gasoline.

Engineers have invented machines that make recycled bottles into winter coats. Sometimes, it is necessary for an engineer to think up a different way of doing things. For instance, engineers imagined houses that could turn off lights when no one is home. Turning off lights that are not being used saves electricity.

Recycled plastic bottles can be made into fleece jackets and other clothing.

THINK ABOUT IT

Think about the things you do every day. Can you think of ways you could save natural resources such as fossil fuels and water?

Rescue workers wash a bird covered in oil.

Now it is time for you to think like an engineer. An oil spill can cause problems for fish, plants, and other living things in or around the water. Large spills can cause problems for people, too. What is the best way to clean up an oil spill?

To find out, put three cups of water in a large bowl. In a small bowl, mix one-half cup of cooking oil with one tablespoon of cocoa powder. Stir the oil and cocoa until they are mixed. The cocoa makes the cooking oil easier to see. Pour the oil and cocoa mix into the water. What do you notice about the oil and water?

Try using a spoon to scoop up the oil. Can you do it without getting any of the water? Next, try using a paper towel to soak up the oil. Does the oil stick to the paper towel? Lastly, put one drop of dishwashing soap on the oil. What do you notice about the oil? Which way cleaned up the oil the best? Can you think of other things you could try to clean up the oil?

Glossary

atmosphere The air surrounding Earth.

carbon dioxide A heavy, colorless gas that traps heat near Earth's surface.

coal A black or brownish black rock that can be burned to make electricity.

electricity A form of energy people use to power lights, fans, and other things in their homes, schools, and businesses.

energy source Something, such as coal, oil, light, heat, or running water, that supplies energy.

engineers People who use their knowledge of science to fix problems.

environment All the physical surroundings on Earth.

filter Something with pores that can sort large objects from small.

gasoline An energy source used to power many machines, such as cars and trucks.

greenhouse effect Warming of Earth's atmosphere caused by gases, such as carbon dioxide, trapping heat from the sun.

green space An area in a city that is filled with trees, grasses, and other plants.

poisonous Causing sickness or death by entering or touching the body.

pollution Waste that destroys or dirties the environment.

renewable energy sources Energy sources, such as sunlight, wind, and water, that cannot be used up.

survive To keep living.

waste Matter that is left over, not wanted, or thrown away; to use more of something than is necessary.

For More Information

Books

Johnson, Robin. *How Engineers Find Solutions*. New York, NY: Crabtree Publishing Co., 2014.

Lawrence, Ellen. *Global Warming*. New York, NY: Bearport Publishing, 2014.

Miller, Reagan. *Engineering in Our Everyday Lives*. New York, NY: Crabtree Publishing Co., 2014.

Miller, Reagan, and Crystal Sikkens. *Engineers Solve Problems*. New York, NY: Crabtree Publishing Co., 2014.

Reynolds, Paul A. *Sydney & Simon: Go Green!* Watertown, MA: Charlesbridge, 2015.

Showers, Paul. *Where Does the Garbage Go?* New York, NY: HarperCollins, 2015.

Websites

Because of the changing nature of Internet links, Rosen Publishing has developed an online list of websites related to the subject of this book. This site is updated regularly. Please use this link to access the list:

http://www.rosenlinks.com/LFO/Green

INDEX